MANGA MYSTERIES

THE SECRET GHOST

A Mystery with Distance and Measurement

by Melinda Thielbar

illustrated by Yuko Ota

Lerner

LERNER BOOKS
NEW YORK · MINNEAPOLIS

SAM
CARTER

MICHELLE
CARTER

AMY
TSANG

TOM
JOHNSON

STACY
LOWICKI

JOY
MEDINA

ADAM BREGMAN

SAM'S DAD

SIGUNG

SIFU FAIZA

What is **distance**? Distance is the space between two points. We can measure distance in inches, feet and miles. We can also measure distance in centimetres, metres and kilometres.

We **measure** to find out the length, size, or weight of something. We use **tools** to measure. We can measure distance with a **ruler** or a **metre ruler** or a **tape measure**. Inches, feet, metres and centimetres are called **units**. A unit can also be the length of your arm or how far you step when you walk.

Story by Melinda Thielbar
Pencils and inks by Yuko Ota
Colouring by Hi-Fi Design
Lettering by Marshall Dillon

First published in the United Kingdom in 2010 by
Lerner Books,
Dalton House,
60 Windsor Avenue,
London SW19 2RR

Website address: www.lernerbooks.co.uk

This edition was edited for UK publication in 2010

A CIP record for this book is available from the British Library

First published in the United States of America in 2010

Printed in China

YOU DO THIS DRILL WITH A BUDDY, SO YOU WANT TO BE FAR ENOUGH AWAY THAT YOU DON'T HIT EACH OTHER.

USE YOUR ARMS TO MEASURE THE DISTANCE. IF YOU'RE TOO FAR AWAY TO TOUCH, YOU'RE TOO FAR AWAY TO HIT.

BUT MAKE SURE YOU EACH MEASURE THE DISTANCE.

BECAUSE IF YOU USE THE SHORTER PERSON'S ARM, THE TALLER PERSON MIGHT HIT THE SHORTER ONE.

IF YOU HAVEN'T DONE THIS BEFORE, FIND A PARTNER WHO HAS.

THANK YOU, SIFU.

6

AWWW... MAN!

TIME! AND THAT'S THE END OF CLASS.

I'VE NEVER SEEN ANYBODY MOVE AS FAST AS SIGUNG! DID YOU SEE HIM KICK THAT BALL?

I WAS TOO BUSY TRYING TO CATCH IT.

SOME OF US ARE STAYING TO HELP PUT UP SOME SHELVES. SAM, DO YOU WANT TO HELP?

ONLY FOR A LITTLE WHILE, ADAM. I'M SUPPOSED TO WALK MY SISTER HOME AFTER HER RIDING LESSON.

AMY, DID I HEAR YOU COUNTING WHILE YOU WERE RUNNING?

YES, TOM.

WHEN WE DO A DRILL, I COUNT MY STEPS. THAT WAY, WHEN I PRACTICE AT HOME IN THE GARDEN, I CAN MEASURE HOW FAR I SHOULD STEP.

BYE, SIFU!

GOOD-BYE! I'LL SEE YOU NEXT TIME.

AND THANK YOU TO THE REST OF YOU FOR STAYING TO HELP.

SAM, ARE YOU LOOKING AT THE METRIC SIDE OF THE TAPE MEASURE?

THE TAPE SAYS 1,219 CM. THE OTHER SIDE SAYS 480 INCHES.

IF SAM IS USING FEET AND INCHES, ADAM MUST HAVE BEEN USING CENTIMETRES. WE'LL STICK WITH CENTIMETRES, SO WE'LL HAVE TO MEASURE AGAIN. WRITE DOWN BOTH, IN CASE THE HARDWARE STORE NEEDS INCHES.

ERASE ERASE ERASE ERASE

measurements for the Room

Width = 300 inches or 762 centimetres
Length = 480 inches or 1,219 centimetres
Perimeter = sum of all sides

762 cm

1,219 cm

THE WIDTH IS 762 CENTIMETRES!

SO, DO WE ADD 762 + 1,219 TO FIND OUT HOW MUCH SHELVING WE NEED?

NOT QUITE, AMY. SAM, DO YOU KNOW WHAT WE SHOULD DO?

THE SCHOOL IS A RECTANGLE, AND WE NEED ALL 4 SIDES.

SO-- DO WE NEED TO MULTIPLY BY 2?

I THINK YOU'RE RIGHT, SAM.

measurements for the Roof

Width= 300 inches or 762 centimetres
Length= 480 inches or 1,219 centimetres
Perimeter= sum of all sides

The school is a rectangle, so:
2 sides are 762 cms.
2 sides are 1,219 cms.

762 cms

1,219 cms

1,219 cms

762 cms

DON'T FORGET ORDER OF OPERATIONS, SIFU. YOU HAVE TO MULTIPLY BEFORE YOU ADD.

48.

THANK YOU, AMY. I'LL DO THE MULTIPLICATION, AND YOU CAN WRITE THE ANSWERS DOWN.

2 X 762 CMS = 1,524 CMS.

2 X 1,219 CMS = 2,438 CMS.

THAT MEANS WE NEED TO ADD 1,524 + 2,438.

1,524 CMS + 2,438 CMS = 3,962 CMS.

DO YOU KNOW WHAT'S MAKING THE NOISES?

IT'S AN OLD HOUSE. IT JUST MAKES NOISE.

IF THE HOUSE IS MAKING LOUD NOISES, THERE MUST BE A REASON.

FAIZA TOLD ME YOU'VE SOLVED MYSTERIES BEFORE. MAYBE YOU CAN FIND OUT WHAT'S MAKING THE NOISES THAT SCARE YOUR SISTER.

YOU KNOW, THERE ARE ALL KINDS OF STORIES ABOUT SHAOLIN MONKS SOLVING MYSTERIES.

WHAT'S A SHAOLIN MONK?

SHAOLIN WAS A BUDDHIST MONASTERY IN CHINA. THAT'S WHERE ALL THE STORIES ABOUT KUNG FU AND FIGHTING MONKS COME FROM.

NOT ALL STORIES ABOUT KUNG FU ARE ABOUT SHAOLIN, BUT A LOT OF THEM ARE. THERE'S ONE THAT REMINDS ME OF YOUR PROBLEM, SAM.

FU HU AND HIS STUDENT SUN JINHUA WERE TRAVELLING TOGETHER.

THEY STOPPED AT AN INN FOR THE NIGHT.

SUN JINHUA IS A GIRL'S NAME. THERE WERE GIRLS IN THE SHAOLIN MONASTERY?

THERE ARE MANY STORIES ABOUT WOMEN WHO KNEW KUNG FU, BUT SUN JINHUA WAS THE FIRST WARRIOR NUN.

OUR WELL IS HAUNTED. WE DON'T GET WATER AFTER DARK.

I APOLOGIZE, GREAT MONK. THERE IS NO WATER FOR YOU TO TAKE A BATH.

HAS YOUR WELL RUN DRY?

OTHER TRAVELLERS WERE AFRAID OF THE GHOST. FU HU AND SUN JINHUA HAD THE INN TO THEMSELVES.

WOOOOOOOOOO

SIFU! IS THAT A GHOST?

I'VE NEVER HEARD A SOUND LIKE THAT, SO I DON'T KNOW WHAT'S MAKING IT.

OOO

OOO

OOOO

SIFU, LOOK!

THAT'S STRANGE. LET'S GET CLOSER.

IT'S GONE!

ASK THE INNKEEPER FOR A LANTERN. I'LL STAY AND WATCH FOR THE GHOST.

PLEASE STAY INSIDE, MISS. I DON'T WANT YOU TO GET HURT.

MY SIFU NEEDS THIS LANTERN. YOU CAN STAY INSIDE IF YOU WISH.

IF THIS LITTLE GIRL ISN'T AFRAID, I CAN'T SHOW FEAR, EITHER.

FU HU PUT THE LANTERN INTO THE BUCKET...

...AND THEN HE LOWERED THE BUCKET INTO THE WELL.

AFTER FU HU CONVINCED THE INNKEEPER THERE WAS NO GHOST, IT WAS PRETTY EASY TO FIND OUT WHO WAS STEALING WATER.

THE HOUSE NEXT TO THE WALL HAD A LARGE GARDEN BUT NO WELL.

THE INNKEEPER HAD OFFERED TO SELL WATER TO HIS NEIGHBOUR, BUT HIS NEIGHBOUR SAID HE HAD ENOUGH WATER.

THE NEIGHBOUR WAS ANGRY WHEN HE WAS ACCUSED OF STEALING.

BUT WHEN HE SAW THAT THE INNKEEPER HAD TWO SHAOLIN MONKS WITH HIM, HE QUICKLY CHANGED HIS ATTITUDE.

ONCE THE INNKEEPER KNEW THERE WASN'T A GHOST, HE WASN'T AFRAID.

SO, IF I SHOW MY SISTER THERE ISN'T A GHOST IN HER ROOM, SHE WON'T BE AFRAID EITHER.

SAM, MAYBE I COULD GO HOME WITH YOU AND HELP YOU WORK OUT WHAT'S CAUSING THE NOISE.

I CAN HELP TOO, IF YOU WANT.

YOU GUYS HELPED ME LAST TIME. I'D LIKE TO HELP YOU IF I CAN.

THAT'S REALLY NICE OF YOU GUYS, BUT I NEED TO LEAVE RIGHT NOW, AND SIFU ISN'T BACK WITH THE SHELVES.

I THINK WE'LL HAVE ENOUGH HELP, EVEN WITHOUT TOM AND AMY. YOU GO AHEAD.

GOOD LUCK!

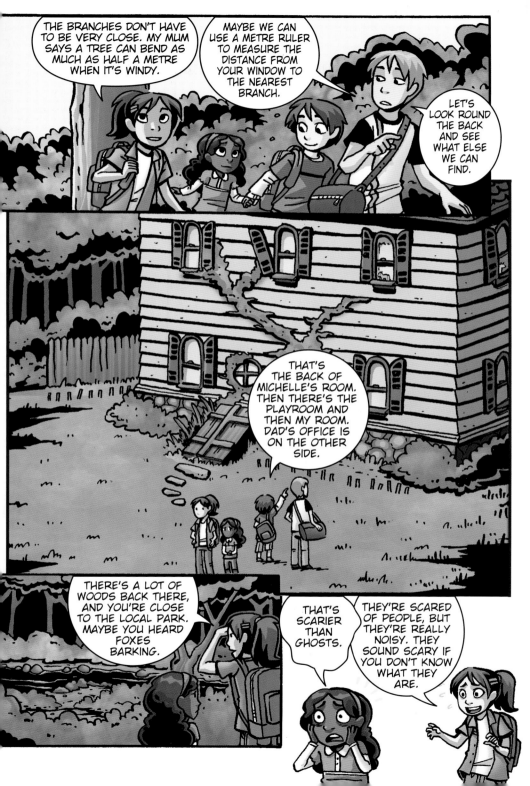

THERE YOU ARE! I'M MAKING PIZZA FOR DINNER. HURRY AND WASH YOUR HANDS OR IT'LL GET COLD.

RACE YOU GUYS INSIDE!

ONE, TWO, THREE, FOUR . . .

. . .FIVE, SIX, SEVEN, EIGHT . . .

I'M GOING TO WIN.

I WIN!

C'MON, SLOW COACHES!

DAD'S STRESSED OUT FROM MOVING. WE DIDN'T WANT TO TELL HIM ABOUT THE GHOST.

MAYBE YOU WON'T HAVE TO AFTER TONIGHT.

THE PIZZA WILL BE READY IN ABOUT 10 MINUTES.

DO YOU GUYS WANT TO EAT IN THE LIVING ROOM SO YOU CAN WATCH A FILM?

CAN WE EAT UPSTAIRS IF WE CLEAN UP AFTER OUR- SELVES?

I GUESS THAT WOULD BE OK, SINCE YOU HAVE FRIENDS OVER.

WHY DON'T YOU TAKE THOSE THINGS UPSTAIRS? I'LL BRING THE PIZZA WHEN IT'S READY.

DAD, DO YOU HAVE A METRE RULER WE CAN USE?

THERE'S ONE BEHIND THE REFRIGERATOR.

IS A METRE RULER LONG ENOUGH?

A METRE RULER SHOULD EASILY BE LONG ENOUGH.

WHAT DO YOU NEED A METRE RULER FOR?

TO MEASURE HOW FAR WE MOVE WHEN WE STEP. WE WERE TALKING ABOUT IT IN KUNG FU CLASS TODAY.

DO YOU THINK HE BELIEVED YOU?

I GUESS SO.

IF THE RULER TOUCHES THE TREE IN LESS THAN HALF A METRE, WE'LL KNOW THE BRANCHES ARE CLOSE ENOUGH TO TAP ON THE WINDOW.

BE SURE TO PUT THE BEGINNING OF THE RULER OUT FIRST.

GOT IT!

THE CLOSEST BRANCH IS 38 CMS AWAY FROM THE WINDOW.

THERE ARE 50 CMS IN HALF A METRE, SO IF WE TAKE 38 CMS FROM 50 CMS, WHAT DOES THAT LEAVE?

The branch is 38 cms away from the window.

Half a metre = 50 cms

50 cms
−38 cms
12 cms

50 − 38 = 12. THAT'S 12 CMS LEFT OVER.

SO, THE BRANCH IS 38 CMS FROM THE WINDOW.

THAT'S A LOT LESS THAN HALF A METRE-- RIGHT?

THAT SOLVES THE MYSTERY, THEN.

FOXES BARKING IN THE BACK GARDEN + TREE BRANCHES TAPPING ON THE WINDOW = SCARY NOISES THAT KEEP MICHELLE AWAKE ALL NIGHT.

NOT ANYMORE!

ARE YOU GUYS READY TO EAT?

MICHELLE

THE END

SAM, WHY DID YOU TURN THE SOUND OFF?

I DON'T LIKE THE MUSIC AT THE END.

BUT IT'S FUN TO WATCH THE OUT-TAKES. EVEN JACKIE CHAN ISN'T PERFECT!

THUMP THUMP

THAT'S NOT TREE BRANCHES!

IT'S THE GHOST!

MAYBE THE NOISES CAME FROM THE PLAYROOM NEXT DOOR.

35

THOSE ARE *BIG* MICE!

ARE YOU GUYS OK?

YEAH, BUT I DON'T WANT TO GO BACK IN THERE.

MAYBE WE DON'T HAVE TO.

I THOUGHT THE GHOST GOT YOU!

I DON'T THINK IT'S A GHOST, MICHELLE.

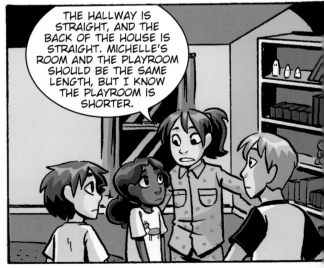

THE HALLWAY IS STRAIGHT, AND THE BACK OF THE HOUSE IS STRAIGHT. MICHELLE'S ROOM AND THE PLAYROOM SHOULD BE THE SAME LENGTH, BUT I KNOW THE PLAYROOM IS SHORTER.

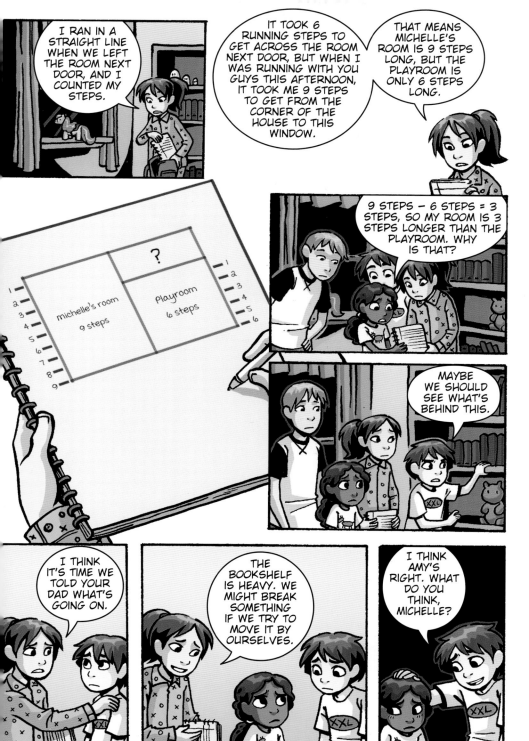

I JUST DON'T WANT DADDY TO BE ANGRY.

I DON'T THINK HE'LL BE ANGRY. LET'S GO DOWN AND TALK TO HIM.

DAD, CAN WE TALK TO YOU?

SURE. WHAT'S UP? YOU TWO LOOK WORRIED.

DADDY, THERE'S A GHOST IN MY ROOM!

...BUT THEN WE HEARD THE NOISES AGAIN, AND AMY SAID WE SHOULD TELL YOU.

I'M GLAD YOU DID. I WANT YOU TO BE HAPPY HERE, AND YOU CAN'T BE HAPPY IF YOU CAN'T SLEEP IN YOUR OWN ROOM.

YOU CAN TELL ME ANYTHING, SWEETHEART.

NOW, I NEED TO GET SOME TOOLS, AND THEN WE CAN GO UPSTAIRS AND FIND YOUR GHOST.

I HEAR IT'S NOISY IN HERE.

YEAH-- A LITTLE.

SAM, TOM, CAN YOU HELP ME MOVE THE BOOKSHELF?

I WAS IN A HURRY TO GET YOUR ROOM READY FOR YOU, MICHELLE.

I DECORATED AND BOUGHT ALL THE FURNITURE.

THIS WALL WAS A LITTLE TATTY, SO I PUT THE BOOKSHELF IN FRONT OF IT. I THOUGHT I'D FIX IT LATER WHILE YOU WERE STAYING WITH YOUR MUM THIS FALL.

THE DOOR WAS NAILED SHUT, SO I DIDN'T WORRY ABOUT IT.

LET'S SEE WHAT'S BEHIND THIS.

C—C—CRACK

DO YOU WANT TO TAKE A LOOK, MICHELLE?

THIS ROOM MUST HAVE BEEN A BATHROOM.

EWWW! IT SMELLS AWFUL IN HERE.

IS THAT A CATFISH?

THUMP THUMP THUMP

HOW MANY CATFISH DID YOUR DAD FIND?

THERE WERE SIX OF THEM. THEY'D BEEN LIVING DOWN IN THE PIPES.

THE OLD BATHROOM HAD A PIPE THAT RAN STRAIGHT OUT TO THE RIVER BEHIND THE HOUSE.

THE THUMPING WAS THE NOISE THEY MADE WHEN THEY SWAM AROUND A BEND IN THE OLD PIPE. IT DID SOUND REALLY CREEPY.

IT WAS REALLY STINKY. AND CATFISH ARE REALLY UGLY.

I'M JUST GLAD WE FOUND OUT WHAT WAS SCARING YOU, MICHELLE.

IT'S GETTING LATE. IF WE'RE GOING TO SWIM, WE'D BETTER GET STARTED.

YOU GUYS GO AHEAD. I'M STILL A BIT TIRED.

CAN I ASK YOU SOMETHING, SAM?

SURE.

THE END